FIRST BULL RUN

THE MACMILLAN BATTLE BOOKS ARE PREPARED UNDER

THE GENERAL EDITORSHIP OF EDWARD R. SAMMIS

FIRST BULL RUN

The Nation Wakes to War

By BRUCE PALMER

THE MACMILLAN COMPANY, NEW YORK
COLLIER–MACMILLAN LIMITED, LONDON

FOR RICK AND DANA

The Macmillan Company, New York
Collier-Macmillan Canada, Ltd., Toronto, Ontario
Library of Congress catalog card number: 65-20511

Picture Credits: Bettmann Archive, page 9; Historical Pictures Service—Chicago, 89; Library of Congress, title page, 6–7, 17 (left), 19, 25, 26, 31, 32, 43, 45, 56, 64, 83, 86, 90; Manassas National Battlefield Park, 11 (buckles); National Archives, 14–15, 92–93; New York Public Library, 53; Radio Times Hulton Picture Library, 12, 23, 34, 36–37, 50, 60, 63, 70, 76–77, 81; John L. Rawls, Vienna, Va., 11 (kepis); Smithsonian Institution, 29, 46; U.S. Army, 17 (right), 67. Picture editing by Gabriele Wunderlich.

Maps by Harry Rosenbaum
Printed in the United States of America
Second Printing, 1966

Contents

The March to Manassas

On April 12, 1861, General Pierre G. T. Beauregard of the Confederate Army opened fire on Fort Sumter, the Federal arsenal built on an island in Charleston Harbor. Within two days, the garrison, short of food and supplies, had surrendered. News of Beauregard's attack and his easy victory flashed to every state in the Union and in the Confederacy.

The American Civil War had begun, a war which struck at the heart of the United States. It would last four long, bitter years, at a cost of half a million lives and billions of dollars in ruined homes, wasted fields, and shattered cities. Before it ended, states fought against each other as well as against the Federal government. In the hills of Kentucky and West Virginia, neighbor fought against neighbor. In many states families were divided. Brother fought against brother; sometimes, fathers against their sons.

No single, simple statement can explain why America divided and then fought. The issue of slavery, so long debated, attacked, and defended, was only one of many.

Both sides were also bitterly and hopelessly divided over the issue of whether or not the states had legal rights superior to those of the Federal government in Washington. They clashed over problems raised by the westward expansion of the American people. Finally, they earned their living in very different ways—a basic difference. The Southern states were essentially agricultural, and depended on their cotton fields and on the price of cotton. However, men of the North were building railroads, great industries, great cities. The

April 12, 1861: Confederate forces open fire on Fort Sumter

Northern city and the Southern plantation could not seem to work for common ends. Every attempt to come together failed at last.

The South Secedes

By the fall of 1860, when Abraham Lincoln was elected President, the time for compromise had passed. Southern politicians knew that this man from the West would not follow the "peace policy" of his predecessor in the presidency. They decided to act on what they felt were their "rights" before Lincoln could take office.

South Carolina took the lead. On December 20, 1860, the state of South Carolina voted to secede. By the light of bonfires and to the sound of bells, she was soon joined by six others from the Deep South: Mississippi, Florida, Alabama, Georgia, Louisiana, and Texas. In a convention held at Montgomery, Alabama, in February, 1861, a provisional government was set up. It adopted a constitution in the name of the Confederate States of America. Jefferson Davis was inaugurated as provisional president of the Confederacy, and the Stars and Bars was chosen as its official flag.

The gauntlet had been thrown down. Would Abraham Lincoln pick it up? Few in either North or South doubted his position. But how would the Federal government act? Would it strike the first blow?

Lincoln still hoped to avoid war. He insisted that secession was unconstitutional, and that the Union was "unbroken." In his inaugural address on March 4, he issued a grave warning to the Southern states: "The government will not assail *you*," he said. "You can have no conflict without being yourselves the aggressors."

Fort Sumter Surrenders

His warning came too late. The Confederacy had already gone too far. At the Montgomery Convention, delegates had passed a resolution to seize Fort Sumter, off the South Carolina coast, and other armories where weapons of war were stored.

While Lincoln and his Cabinet argued about how to relieve the beleaguered fort, General Beauregard received his instructions. He ordered its commander, Major Anderson, to surrender. Anderson refused. Beauregard's shore batteries opened fire. Gaily dressed men and women watched from the shore as if this were a sham battle. The fort could not be defended, and Major Anderson surrendered to Beauregard, his former student at West Point.

Yankee blue and Rebel gray: insignia of the opposing armies

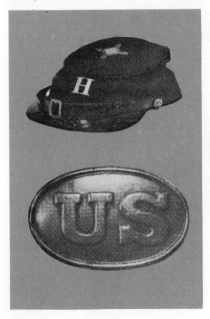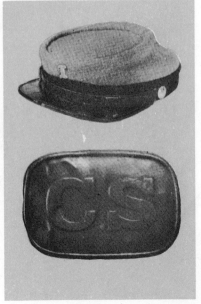

Anxious New York citizens crowd together to read the war news

The Call for Volunteers

Fort Sumter was a cry of jubilation in the South, but in Washington it was a name that rankled. Public opinion was soon further aroused by the loss of other Federal forts and arsenals, storehouses of war strength. Many of these, located in states that had seceded, were easily taken over by the Confederacy. Both sides called for volunteers, and the Confederacy, now joined by Virginia, North Carolina, Tennessee, and Arkansas, moved its capital to Richmond, only 100 miles from Washington.

Two days after Sumter fell, President Lincoln called for 75,000 volunteers "to put down the rebellion." The Regular Army numbered less than 16,000 men, so the call went out to the loyal states to form militia units of volunteers. The response was immediate, and all through the spring these men assembled in Washington for training. They were also expected to protect the capital, which was almost surrounded by Rebel states.

Volunteers flocked to the cause of the Confederacy, too. They came from Arkansas and Texas, from Georgia, Mississippi, Tennessee, Alabama, Louisiana, Virginia, and both Carolinas. They came from the backwoods and from the large plantations. They came on foot and on horseback. Some were veterans of the Mexican War. Some carried weapons they had used against the Indians or to hunt wild game. Their officers were often West Pointers, classmates of the Union commanders.

Most of the soldiers who camped around the two capitals had signed up for short terms of enlistment—some for a period no longer than ninety days. Both sides hoped for a very brief war.

Ninety days. Three months. Not a long time to fight a war, although a busy time for the tailors who cut and sewed uniforms for the new recruits. Orders had been issued in the North and South for regulation field or battle dress. The Union troops would wear the blue jackets and trousers which were standard in the Federal Army. The Confederates chose gray. The militia units, volunteers from many states, seldom resisted their desire for splendid colors. The price of plumes, silk tassels, and gold braid rose sharply.

Of the two armies so swiftly assembled, the Confederates took up a better position. Twenty thousand Rebel soldiers were camped in tents and huts at Manassas Junction, only 30 miles from Washington. At this strategic spot, where two railroads met, the Rebel forces dug themselves in behind ramparts of heaped-up earth and logs. Not only did their encampment screen their new capital at Richmond from attack, but it was a threat to Washington, the Union capital.

On a clear day, from any convenient hill, the Southern officers and men could see the city where the Union Army was gathering. With a good pair of field glasses, the Rebel commander, Pierre Gustave Toutant Beauregard, could even see the unfinished iron dome of the Capitol Building itself.

Only two months earlier, General Beauregard had directed Carolina militia in the successful attack on Fort Sumter in Charleston Harbor. Soon he expected to be joined at Manassas by an additional 9,000 troops stationed 50 miles away, up the Potomac River, under General Joseph E. Johnston. If necessary, Johnston could rush his men by forced march and then by railroad to join Beauregard.

Rebel fortifications near Manassas, 30 miles from Washington

The Nation's War Cry

While the Rebels dug in at Manassas in a growing threat to Washington, in June, 1861, the streets of the capital were crammed with thousands of three-month volunteers who had nearly served out their time. Before they returned to their home states, they were eager to prove themselves in battle, to wipe out the loss of Sumter and other garrisons.

News from the border states added fuel to the flames of patriotism. In West Virginia, General George B. McClellan had scattered two small Rebel forces at Philippi and Rich Mountain. The newspapers inflated the victory, quoting McClellan's boast that he had "annihilated two armies. . . ."

Editors called for action. If McClellan could win with

raw troops in the mountains, why wait longer to shatter the cocky Confederates and restore the Union?

No newspaper spoke with a louder voice than the New York *Daily Tribune*. Each morning on the front page appeared a feature which the editor, Horace Greeley, called "The Nation's War Cry." He urged an offensive:

Forward to Richmond! Forward to Richmond! The Rebel Congress must not be allowed to meet there on the 20th of July. By that date the place must be held by the National Army.

These were strong words, and stirring as well, to people hungry for good news. It seemed so simple. All the Union needed was a great victory. One hammer stroke and the war would be over, with little loss of life.

Every day, with no regard for military secrecy, the newspapers printed maps showing the troop positions. The government was bombarded with suggestions by impatient civilians and armchair strategists:

Why not pack up the Army of the Potomac and run them out to Manassas by train?

Or, if there was danger of Rebel dynamiters blowing up the railroad tracks and trestles, why not send the army on foot? It wasn't far. What was 25 or 30 miles? There were good roads all the way from the capital to Manassas.

Others argued that the Army of the Potomac could be divided. Some could go by train, others on foot.

The public ear caught the wild cries of the newspapers. The public voice began to murmur and then to roar: "On to Richmond! On to Richmond!"

No government, no president or cabinet could long resist such a clamor without losing support and public confidence. Lincoln himself, that gaunt and lanky man from

LEFT: *General Irvin McDowell, commander of the Union troops*
RIGHT: *General Pierre G. T. Beauregard, Confederate commander*

Illinois, had promised all the listening world that he meant to preserve the Union. If the Union proved unable to control the Rebels, there was danger that England might decide to recognize and support the Confederacy. British mills had large interests in Southern cotton.

The war cries grew louder. Action was demanded. Should it be "on to Richmond"?

McDowell's Battle Plan

Lincoln called his Cabinet and several generals together on June 29, 1861. Old General Winfield Scott, supreme commander of the Union Armies, had already publicly announced his views. He favored a massive build-up of strength, then a slow, crunching advance down the Mississippi Valley. Lincoln rejected the plan at once. This was no time for long-range tactics. The meeting had been called to decide on the best system for knocking Beauregard out of Manassas.

Scott nudged General Irvin McDowell, a veteran of the Mexican War of 1845. McDowell presented his battle plan. He would move the Union Army against Manassas in three columns. The first would occupy the town of Fairfax Court House. The second would attack along the Little River Road. The third would be shipped into action along the Orange and Alexandria Railroad line.

McDowell was aware of the many difficulties. He was fully aware of the Rebel spies who haunted Washington and the north bank of the Potomac River. He warned the President and Cabinet: "We cannot count on keeping secret our intentions . . . they [the spies] are alive and well-informed as to every movement, however slight, we make."

A professional soldier, McDowell saw other obstacles that no civilian or newspaper editor noticed. East of Manassas Junction was a small river that meandered in lazy loops, its sloping banks choked with willows, cattails, and weeds. The Army of the Potomac would have to cross this natural barrier, and there was only one narrow bridge.

The name of the river was Bull Run.

The Army of the Potomac was made up of 35,000 men—infantry, artillery, and cavalry. A force of such size could not pass over a single, small bridge. McDowell was not discouraged. He had never seen the little river, but men who knew it had told him that the water was shallow. The Union general was reasonably confident that the river would not halt or delay his attack on Beauregard.

A general with eyes as sharp as McDowell's looks at men as well as maps. His green troops would have their hands full with the 20,000 Rebels already assembled under Beauregard. He was just as anxious that Johnston's Rebels up the Potomac, 9,000 men, should *not* join Beauregard, as Beauregard hoped that they would. If the two Rebel armies could be kept apart, then the Union Army would outnumber the Confederates at Manassas by a comfortable margin.

McDowell needed every advantage he could get. His own army presented a serious problem. He knew it for what it was—an army in name only. In reality, the Union Army was a gathering of restless amateurs, untrained for war. Most of the volunteers seemed to look on a soldier's life as a com-

A Federal cavalryman before battle (drawing by Edwin Forbes)

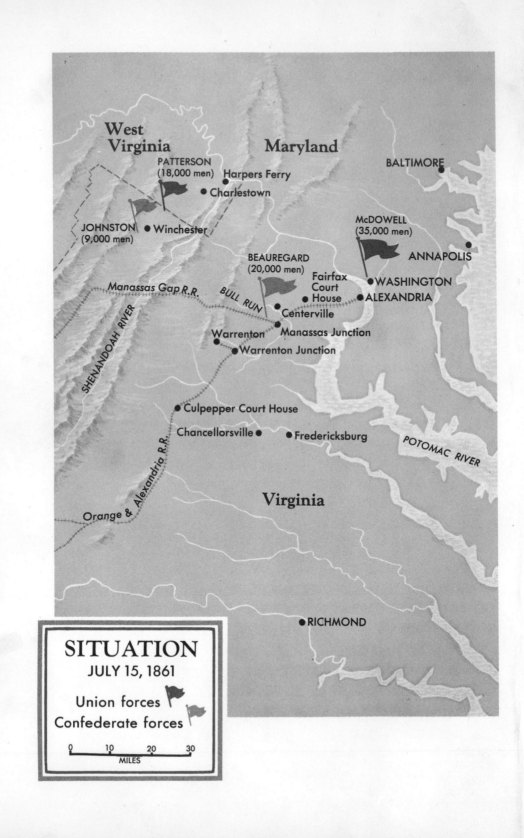

West
Virginia

Maryland

PATTERSON
(18,000 men)
● Harpers Ferry
● Charlestown

BALTIMORE

JOHNSTON
(9,000 men) ● Winchester

McDOWELL
(35,000 men)

ANNAPOLIS

BEAUREGARD
(20,000 men)

Fairfax
Court
House

WASHINGTON

Manassas Gap R.R.

BULL RUN

Centerville

ALEXANDRIA

SHENANDOAH RIVER

Warrenton ● Manassas Junction
● Warrenton Junction

● Culpepper Court House

Chancellorsville ● ● Fredericksburg

POTOMAC RIVER

Orange & Alexandria R.R.

Virginia

●RICHMOND

SITUATION
JULY 15, 1861

Union forces
Confederate forces

0   10   20   30
MILES

bination of vacation and camping trip. Few knew more than the simplest military drill. They had fired their rifles only at fixed targets. They had never used a bayonet.

Even the quality of the officers was cause for deep concern. Most were West Point graduates, like McDowell himself, but in the haste to raise an army quickly, promotions had been made too rapidly. Lieutenants and captains had become majors and colonels in charge of brigades. They commanded units larger than their skills or training warranted. Only Ricketts' regular artillery and a portion of the infantry were in any sense ready for a major battle.

McDowell begged Lincoln for time. He urged him to forget the pressures from the public and the newspapers. Weeks must pass before the gang of uniformed civilians could become an organized fighting force.

Lincoln nodded when he read McDowell's words. What his general had written was very true. However, the ninety-day recruits would soon be going home. Then the whole process of training volunteer troops would have to be started all over again. Lincoln wrote to McDowell: "You are green, it is true; but they are green also. You are all green alike."

McDowell received his orders on the ninth day of July. He was granted seven days to make final preparations. Then the army must move against Beauregard.

Confederate Spies

The Union general had not exaggerated the activities and cleverness of the Confederate spies in Washington. The two capitals were only 100 miles apart. The battle lines were not tightly drawn, and no attempt as yet had been made to control what was printed in the newspapers.

July 16 was officially set as the day for McDowell's troops
to move. That very morning, a Rebel sympathizer, who was
working as a clerk in a Washington office, sat down to break-
fast in his lodgings four blocks from the White House. He
was served by a woman, also a spy, who had regular contact
with Richmond. She transcribed this message into code:
ORDER ISSUED FOR MCDOWELL TO MARCH ON MANASSAS TO-
NIGHT.

The clerk swilled down his coffee, stuffed the note into
his boot, and hurried to his horse. The Union Army had
already gathered to pass in review on its way out of Washington. But there was no one to stop the messenger as he
hurried to his destination.

Review of the Union Troops

The march to Manassas was about to begin. General Mc-
Dowell drew on his white cotton gloves and nodded to the
bugler. The bugler wet his lips and set them stiff against the
mouthpiece of his instrument. As the brisk notes echoed off
the stone housefronts, the officers mounted, adjusted their
stirrups, and folded their reins. The general nodded and
urged his horse forward.

The bugle blared again, and the flag-bearers raised their
long wooden lances with the colored pennants flying from
their tips. Down the long line the commands were passed.

The Union Army, bright as a great Chinese dragon,
marched forward. Up went the regimental colors. Polished
sticks thundered on taut drumheads. Cymbals clashed. All
the bands sounded off together.

The streets of Washington had been cleared, but the side-
walks were packed with a huge, cheering crowd. Banners

and bunting hung from open windows. Excited boys waved their caps and shouted from chimneys and rooftops.

Rank on rank, the Union Army marched along under the hot sun, stirring up the dust in the wide streets. Most colorful of all were the Zouaves from New York. They were dressed in baggy red breeches, snow-white gaiters, and shiny black boots. Their tight blue jackets were sashed with yellow silk, and on their heads bobbed small turbans with black tassels. Their uniforms were patterned after those of the famous French colonial troops.

Following them came the 39th New York—called the Garibaldi Guards, after the Italian patriot. They moved at double time, a swift trot, the long plumes in their soft felt hats shining green and silver.

The 2d Wisconsin, a long way from home, were smartly uniformed in gray, a tragic choice of color. Scores of the red-faced, grinning troopers now mopping their brows under the hot sun would be shot by their own comrades, who

Amid cheering crowds, McDowell's soldiers leave Washington

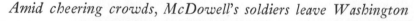

would confuse them with the enemy Rebels in the dust and chaos of battle.

Small children shrank back against their parents' knees and stared wide-eyed as Ricketts' Federal artillery rumbled past. The powerful horses moved easily in teams of four, hauling the brass cannon and ammunition wagons. The gunners sat stiffly, grim and unsmiling. They were veterans of the Mexican War. They knew their trade, the flesh-scorching, powder-black business of long-range killing with shell and solid shot.

A cheer swept through the crowd as a drum and bugle corps went by, the deep drums pounding out the rhythm. Behind them marched a triple line of young boys, playing a bright and skipping tune on sparkling silver fifes. The youngsters on the rooftops were hot with envy.

And then . . . the cavalry! Their horses were handsome and well-groomed. Their uniforms were blue and red, with plenty of gold braid and shining brass buttons. Their heavy sabers flashed against the blue saddle blankets stamped *U.S.* at the corners. The riders waved and laughed as they bent to catch the flowers tossed to them by pretty girls.

There was no laughter when Colonel William Tecumseh Sherman, a fire-eater from the West, passed by. The crowd knew him, a grim-faced man with a grizzled red beard and blue piercing eyes, who hated all newspaper reporters and kept threatening to have them jailed as spies. He knew that war was to be taken seriously. Now he turned in the saddle and signaled to the officers of his brigade to dress the lines, to keep the men in even ranks.

On and on they came: men from Massachusetts, New Jersey and Connecticut, Rhode Island and Maine. The dust boiled into a choking cloud, and still they passed by, thou-

Drawing of a Union artillery wagon used during the Civil War

sand after thousand, while the bands played and the flags whipped in the hot sunshine. More cavalry, more cannon, more marching men with bayonets glittering like needles of death. Then came carts and more carts, to carry all the important supplies for an army on the march, an endless baggage train loaded with food, water, ammunition, tents, copper coils of telegraph wire, and other necessities. Last of all came the plain, canvas-topped wagons that would carry away the wounded and the dying, although nobody wanted to think about that.

Men and women, boys and girls cheered and waved until their arms ached and their throats were parched. The slam and bang of drums faded away as the Union Army crossed the Long Bridge and moved into enemy Virginia. The wagons rumbled off and the sounds died away across the river. Friend and foe alike knew their objective—Manassas.

As the crowds turned toward home, newsboys with their shrill cries began hawking the special editions heaped in bundles on every street corner. One paper took it for granted that the great victory the North was hoping for had already been won on the muddy banks of Bull Run:

Our brave army moves toward Manassas, and thence—we hope without delay—to RICHMOND! The fever's up, and our bold troops ask only to be led, and listen earnestly for the thrilling order—*forward!*

The Road to Battle

The Union Army left Washington and the cheers and the flowers and the pretty girls behind them. The bands stopped playing. After that, there were only the baking sun, the dust, and the endless road up over Arlington Heights and out through the lazy countryside.

A footsore volunteer rests during the long march to Manassas

The sounds of the march were thousands of boots scuffing in the dust, thousands of steel-shod hooves clinking on stones. The dust rose in choking clouds around the troops, drifting into their eyes, noses, and throats.

The men began to slow down. Their new boots rubbed blisters on their tender feet. Their packs seemed to be loaded with stones instead of food and bedding. Their shoulder straps worked loose, and the packs flopped heavily from side to side. Their rifles grew heavier with every mile, and their empty canteens rattled tantalizingly against the cartridge boxes on their sweat-soaked belts.

Even in the hottest weather, they had never known anything like this in camp, where their hours of drill had been interrupted by rest periods in the shade at the edge of the parade grounds.

Now, on the road to battle, the few experienced "regulars" were not enough to hold together the huge "awkward squad" of raw recruits who made up the larger part of the marching columns. The army was still in sight of Washington when the men began to falter.

At first it was only a man here, another there. With no respect for discipline, they called out to the nearest sergeant that they were breaking ranks, and then dropped out of formation. A Zouave flung himself down to gasp for breath and to claw open his tight little jacket soaked with sweat. A private in the 5th Maine dropped his rifle, took three long, loose-jointed strides, and flopped in the dust, unconscious from sunstroke. Two of his comrades dropped out to help him. They were tired, anyway. They sat by the roadside in the shade and pulled off their boots.

A corporal from a New York regiment coughed and coughed from the dust that sifted into his lungs. He blinked the stinging sweat from his eyes. He coughed again and clopped one hand to his face. Blood gushed from his nose. He dropped out of line and searched desperately for cold water. When he found a stream at last thirty men were there ahead of him, filling their canteens.

When the army stopped to eat, the soldiers collapsed as though their legs were made of wax. The bugles called to re-form and resume march, but large numbers of men stayed right where they were. They did not mean to disobey orders, but they were exhausted. Officers tried to be both firm and sympathetic at the same time. The men groaned and stood up, ready to march. When an officer hurried off to report his group as ready, the men sat down again and fanned their faces with their caps.

Everyone was tired, hot, and footsore. The horses stirred up the dried roads, especially the artillery and ammunition wagons with their four- and six-horse hitches. In Keyes' and Richardson's brigades, the lines melted. Where a company had marched in the morning, now only three men shuffled along, sucking at empty canteens. Others tried tying bandannas over their faces. It kept out some of the dust, but it was hard to breathe through the folds.

A man from Sherman's brigade spotted some blackberries growing in the shade. He slipped away and scrambled up the bank, took off his cap, and began to pick. The place was a real find. Thousands of the sweet, juicy berries grew wild beneath the trees. Within half an hour, fifty others came to help him pick.

The pace slowed to a crawl. The heat was cruel to the animals, too. Swarms of flies settled on their lathered skins. The horses whisked their tails and kicked at the traces. The troopers kept a constant watch for water. When the horses

Hardtack and eating utensils used by the men of the Union army

smelled it, they bolted toward it, as desperate for a drink as the foot soldiers. The officers grew short-tempered. They warned the men: any trooper who let his weary and over-heated mount get the belly-bloat would answer for it.

It got hotter and hotter as the army straggled along the road. Entire companies dropped out of line, a hundred men at a time. The officers had been elected by popular vote. They didn't want to be too hard on the men who had voted them gold braid and higher rank. Too often they granted permission to break ranks and rest.

Roadside ditches began to gather the litter of the march. In an agony of discomfort, the men stripped off the uniforms that had seemed so fine back on the parade ground. They dropped their haversacks and blanket rolls, promising them-selves they'd come back for them later, when the army halted for the night. They mopped their sweating faces as they looked for the nearest stream. They stumbled forward on aching legs, wondering: How far to Fairfax Court House? How far to Manassas? The army dragged along miserably as the sun went down. At the end of the first day's march, only a few brigades had reached Fairfax Court House; Manassas was still a long way.

The men of the Union Army could hardly eat. There was no way to escape the dust. It rose up above the trees in a cloud, and then settled down on the frying bacon and the bubbling stew. It left a film of grit on the coffee. Most of all, the men craved water and rest. They forgot about their castoff equipment. They poked at their blistered feet and joked about putting in for a wound stripe.

The men cursed Beauregard as much as the weather. Why couldn't he have put his army somewhere handy, instead of making a fellow traipse all over the hot countryside to find him?

General Patterson's Mistake

While the main force of the Federal troops was struggling and sweating on its march to Manassas, General Robert Patterson, in charge of Union troops between Manassas and Harpers Ferry, was about to make a serious mistake. Patterson did not like his position: pushed across the Potomac into the Shenandoah Valley. He did not like the local Rebel population. He did not like the thought of Johnston's Rebel force only nine miles away. Especially he did not like his new orders: press Johnston hard and make him fight. Nor did he like the idea that General McDowell, nearly thirty years his junior, was his superior in command.

Fairfax Courthouse, where the Union volunteers spent the night

When the bugler sounded taps over Patterson's encampment on the evening of July 16, the general felt exhausted, tired out by the fierce heat that had lasted all day and spoiled his appetite. It spoiled his judgment, too. He had readied his force to punch at Johnston's position. Now he would call them back.

General Patterson laid three large sheets of paper out on his table and dipped the steel nib of his pen into the inkwell. He wrote as his mind worked, slowly, cautiously, each letter elegant and spidery, the lines set close together. He ordered his advance guard, already in position to check Johnston, to move to Charlestown—*away* from the Rebel force. When he signed his name to that order, Patterson made it possible for Johnston to join Beauregard at Manassas.

Breaking camp (*engraving from the* New York Illustrated News)

Now all the Confederate commander nine miles away needed was the order to move. And at one o'clock in the morning, July 18, the telegraph key sparked and chattered, and this telegram was delivered to Johnston:

General Beauregard is attacked; to strike the enemy a decisive blow, a junction of all your effective force will be needed. If practicable, make the movement, sending your sick and baggage to Culpepper Court House either by railroad or Warrenton. In all the arrangements, exercise your discretion.

(signed) General Cooper,
Adjutant and Inspector General

General Johnston on the Move

Without delay, Johnston moved to join Beauregard. He moved his troops, at forced-march pace, to the railroad sidings where freight cars were waiting. He knew there was no time to lose.

The Rebels found the sun just as hot, the dust as dry and choking, the water as scarce and delicious, as the Federal Army had found on their march out of Washington. Blackberries tempted the Rebel troops too, but their leader had been a minister before the war, and he kept them from giving in to temptation. He wrote later: "The discouragement of that day's march to one accustomed, like myself, to the steady gait of regular soldiers, is indescribable."

At last the sun set and Johnston gave the order to halt. Officers swabbed the dust off their horses and went back to round up their men. It was like herding sheep. The soldiers bleated and ducked off into the bushes. Johnston shook his head. They had covered only half the distance he had planned.

Confederate soldiers pass in review before General Beauregard

Like all strangers traveling together, the soldiers talked mostly about the weather:

"Hot enough for you, brother?"

"Hot as the hinges of hell and twice as dusty!"

The next day was worse. Johnston's Rebels hung in the shade at the roadside and slouched along, while their officers kept assuring them that they were getting closer to the railroad depots every minute. The men nodded glumly.

A Time of Waiting

Meanwhile, General Beauregard waited at Manassas Junction, but not patiently. He was not a patient man. Where in heaven's name was Johnston's force? And where, exactly, was McDowell and the enemy?

The Rebel commander reviewed his troops. He ordered the sick to the rear and set about strengthening his defenses. If the men were kept busy, they would worry less about the coming battle. Waiting is hard on any soldiers, and hardest of all on green troops. Any experienced general knew that.

Beauregard rode up and down his lines. He shifted companies of infantry in skirmish lines fifty paces closer to Bull Run. He sent more ammunition up to the cannon he had planted at Stone Bridge to block the highway. The waiting Rebels were told to stay under cover of bushes and trees and watch out for Yankee cavalry. The roads west of Bull Run were sprinkled to keep down some of the dust.

Another day went by. Beauregard sent a rider down regularly to the telegraph office at the railroad junction to ask after the troop train that was now overdue. Where was Johnston? Where were the Union troops under McDowell?

Both armies were still limping and panting and struggling through the drifting dust beneath the scorching sun to reach Manassas. It had taken General McDowell two full days to drive his army thirty miles. Shortly after noon on July 18, a Federal cannon belched smoke, and a shell wailed across the pale hot sky. It blasted the chimney and part of the roof off a house near Manassas Junction.

The small, handsome man seated at the dining-room table eating his lunch blinked slowly, scrubbed his mustache with his napkin, and stood up. The time of waiting was over for Beauregard.

Ten days earlier, the Confederate hero of Fort Sumter had written: "If I could only get the enemy to attack me, I would stake my reputation on the handsomest victory that could be hoped for."

Beauregard knew that McDowell had arrived. His former classmate from West Point had come to provide the flamboyant Rebel with the chance to do battle on a field of his own choosing.

Would the Confederate general be able to make good his boast of a handsome victory?

2.

The Battle Is Joined

Advance units of General McDowell's army had reached the vicinity of Bull Run by July 18, but they were not yet ready for battle. The main units were being regrouped around Centerville, while many stragglers were still some distance back, pounding along in the dust or trying to find their brigades.

McDowell wanted certain facts before he could go ahead with his battle plan. He needed to know more about the depth of the water in the little river of Bull Run. He needed to know the strength of Beauregard's position. While the rest of the army regrouped, he sent a division forward to get this information. Could men and horses wade across Bull Run? Was the footing in the stream bed sandy, stony, or muddy? Was Bull Run going to be an obstacle or simply a place to get wet feet?

A full brigade is not a scouting party. More than a thousand men went out. The blue infantry was supposed to make noise, to draw attention to their presence, but to avoid a pitched battle. With luck, they might take a few prisoners. They did not realize that they were too far forward and that the Rebels would obviously be guarding the shallow places. At Blackburn's Ford, they crashed down the bank, right into the center of the Rebel line.

The gray sharpshooters were ready, crouched behind trees and shrubs. They held their fire as the Yankees blundered within range. They waited until the sword arms of their commanders flashed in downstroke—the signal to fire. Then rifles spat and crackled. Powder smoke hung over the dense bushes. Bullets whipped across the ford and thudded into the startled Union troops. Leaves shredded from the trees, and their shot-cut limbs sagged down on the milling soldiers.

The Yankees returned the fire, a ragged volley aimed blindly into the drifting smoke across the stream. Bullets bounced off the sun-baked stones and splashed into the water.

Across the stream, the Rebels reloaded. Safe in the shelter of the undergrowth, they fumbled with paper cartridges, bit off the waxed ends with their teeth, and spilled the loose grains of powder down the muzzles of their rifles. Ramrods clinked as the lead bullets were driven down and snugged. The little percussion caps were slipped over the nipples, and the hammers clicked up to cock. Down came the sword arms again; again the rifle butts slugged against the shoulders of the hidden men as they discharged a second volley.

This volley had artillery support. A Confederate battery of four guns banged away. Shells split in mid-air, spraying the blue soldiers with iron fragments.

Yankee voices bawled orders, and the Union infantry staggered back up the slope. Blue bodies slumped, moaning, in the torn weeds and cattails. Others lay motionless in the slow stream, their rifles half sunk in the silt. The waters were tinged with blood.

Beauregard nodded with satisfaction as his field officers came up to report the action at Blackburn's Ford. He grinned, his white teeth shining beneath his mustache. Troops under his command had drawn the first blood of the war at Fort Sumter. Now they had drawn blood again. It was a good sign. Beauregard summoned his staff officers for a council.

The staff meeting was attended by Generals Barnard E. Bee, James Longstreet, Richard S. Ewell, and Thomas J. Jackson. Johnston, who outranked Beauregard, had not yet

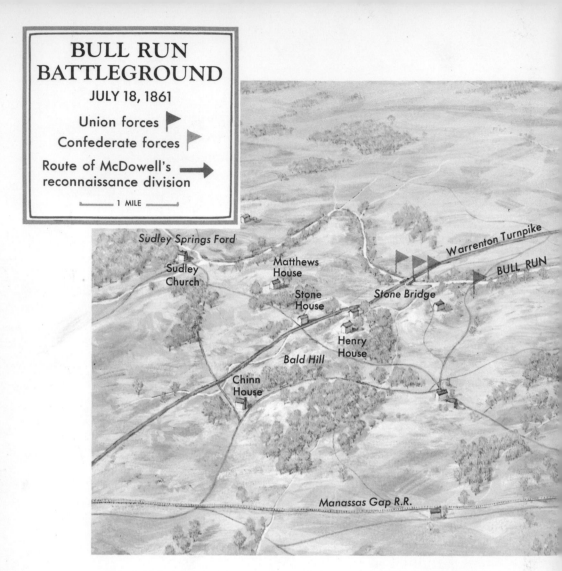

BULL RUN BATTLEGROUND

JULY 18, 1861

Union forces ▶
Confederate forces ▶
Route of McDowell's reconnaissance division ➡

1 MILE

Sudley Springs Ford

Sudley Church

Matthews House

Stone House

Bald Hill

Chinn House

Henry House

Stone Bridge

Warrenton Turnpike

BULL RUN

Manassas Gap R.R.

arrived. Beauregard gestured with his small, elegant hands as he outlined his battle plan. It was an elaborate one, modeled on the flank attack used by Napoleon in his sensational victory at Austerlitz.

Perhaps it is not surprising that a man with a name as grand as Pierre Gustave Toutant Beauregard and a reputation as a hero should think of himself as a potential Napoleon. They shared a common French heritage, and Beauregard did not attempt to conceal his admiration for the military genius who

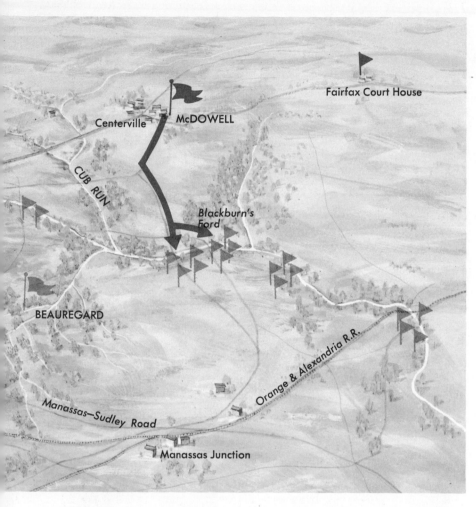

had conquered most of Europe fifty years earlier. Besides, the students at West Point all studied the tactics of Napoleon.

So Beauregard explained his plan. The Confederate Army lay along Bull Run for nearly eight miles. Certain units had been concentrated at Stone Bridge and at the fords where McDowell would have to cross. But Napoleon had not waited at Austerlitz, and Beauregard had been waiting for the best part of a week. He planned to strike the Union force before it was ready to fight. It was no secret that the green troops under McDowell had not yet recovered from their grueling march from Washington.

Beauregard was quite vain, but he was not foolish. Much as he was tempted to attack at once, his common sense prompted him to wait for Johnston. Not only would the reinforcements be welcome, but Johnston was his superior and would not be pleased to have the battle begun before he arrived.

Still fuming over the slow march and the slower railroad connections, Johnston finally arrived on July 20. He did not bring with him his whole force. He had hurried to join Beauregard, leaving the stragglers to follow under General Edmund Kirby-Smith and Colonel Jubal Early.

On his arrival, Johnston automatically assumed command, placing Beauregard in an awkward position. Johnston's brigade leaders hardly knew Beauregard's field commanders. The two groups were poorly coordinated. Sober, dignified Johnston was a different sort of man from the gallant, impetuous Beauregard. Now that the two groups were joined, Beauregard explained the tactics of his proposed flank attack.

The Confederate Battle Plan

The first move in Beauregard's battle plan would be a feint, like the left jab of a boxer. It would not be a solid punch —just enough of a thrust to throw the enemy off balance. Then the Confederate right wing would cross the shallow stream under strong covering fire and fall upon the side, or flank, of the Union force.

It was a good plan. In war, as in the prize ring, it is always a good plan to hit the opponent from the side when he is not looking. But it was a plan that needed a well-trained army with some experience in both feint and flank attack. It needed good communication between staff and field officers. It needed enough open ground so that troops could be maneuvered with some freedom.

The key to a successful flank attack is speed as well as brute force. There was nothing along the bramble-choked banks of Bull Run that resembled the fields at Austerlitz. The Rebel troops, like McDowell's, were for the most part poorly trained volunteers.

General Johnston was not very enthusiastic about Beauregard's Austerlitz plan. Johnston was an expert at *defensive* warfare. Later he would practice the tactics of the wolf: dash and rip and run away; turn back, rip again, and run away. But the warfare of the wolf demands detailed knowledge of

A drawing from life of one of the men who fought at Bull Run

the terrain, and Johnston had never studied the hills, gaps, and woodlands along Bull Run. It was Beauregard, not Johnston, who knew every farmhouse on the banks of the river and along the Warrenton Turnpike. A compromise battle plan was finally worked out.

Beauregard would actually command in the field, a decision based on common sense and courtesy. He agreed, however, to delay any attack of the Austerlitz variety until the remainder of Johnston's army appeared. The strategy to be used was settled. The Rebel attack was scheduled to begin at eight o'clock on Sunday morning, July 21.

There was a third strategist present at this war council meeting who would play a deciding role in the battle to come, but who said nothing now. He was Beauregard's brigadier, T. J. Jackson, leader of the Virginia troops. At one time, he had been a minister like Johnston; at another a professor of tactics at Virginia Military Institute, the nation's second-ranking war college. Jackson wore a full beard and had such piercing blue eyes that his soldiers called him "Old Blue Lights." By Sunday night, he would have a new nickname.

The Union Battle Plan

While the Confederate generals were discussing battle strategy, General McDowell was doing the same thing. A West Pointer like Beauregard, and a graduate of the same year, McDowell, not surprisingly, also was planning a flank attack modeled on the carefully studied strategy of Napoleon. In brief, the Union general's battle plan was the Rebel scheme, in reverse.

One difference between the two plans was that there was no question of rank at Union headquarters. The only pro-

LEFT: *Confederate General Joseph E. Johnston.* RIGHT: *Brigadier General Thomas J. Jackson, commander of the Virginia Brigade*

test was raised by Colonel William Tecumseh Sherman, who wanted his brigade to take part in the main attack, rather than serve in a supporting position. General McDowell politely refused. The meeting was terminated, and McDowell's battle plan was endorsed by his staff officers: Richardson, Schenck, Keyes, Heintzelman, and Sherman. McDowell would lead the flank attack in person.

The Union commander knew that there was no element of surprise in his plan. He would simply have to do the best he could, using his few experienced units where they would be the most effective. The hour of the attack was set. In the meantime, he flung out a line of his most dependable infantry-men as pickets or observation units. They kept up a harassing fire across the river, but always broke off and slid away before the Rebel artillery could locate them.

After the long, hot march from Washington, the Army of the Potomac had finally shambled together in fairly good order. The many units found their assigned positions, more

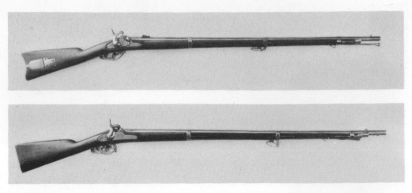

TOP: *A Union rifle-musket.* BOTTOM: *A Confederate musket*

or less. It was a task made easier by the differences between their uniforms. At least the fancy clothes were good for something, if not for marching on a summer's day.

Behind them lay 30 miles of road with the dust standing high in the still, hot air like the smoke of a vast forest fire. The blackberries had been stripped from every handy bush, and many soldiers scratched grimly at fresh cases of poison ivy. They were short of food and blankets, but they had finally made it to Manassas.

The Union Army was a tired army, though, unlike the fresh troops across the river. McDowell realized this, but he could not afford to wait. He issued his orders. The men were to be awakened at two o'clock in the morning, fed promptly, and ready to fight at dawn.

That night, the soldiers tried to find a few square feet of comfort on the bare ground. Many went hungry if they could not borrow food from their more practical or better disciplined comrades. Others cursed themselves for throwing away their blankets. They hung over the flaring fires and swatted at mosquitoes. Later, as they tossed restlessly on the uncomfortable ground, they wondered whether on the next night they might be sleeping beneath the torn sod.

Unwelcome Guests

One of the most unusual and unwelcome aspects of the battle which would take place on Sunday, July 21, 1861, was the presence of an eager crowd of spectators. The battle had been as well advertised as a medieval tournament or modern sports event. There was no secret about the time or place. The lure of blood had attracted sight-seers from the Union capital. They came in gigs, carts, carriages, and on riding horses. Congressmen and senators came dressed in frock coats and frilled shirts; clearly, they expected the forthcoming skirmish to be a great occasion.

The sight-seers came out to see the battle fought, and they brought their wives and friends, even their children and nursemaids. They brought out picnic hampers and tablecloths. They brought cold meats, bread, fruit, wine, and expensive cigars.

The hills to the east of Bull Run form a sort of natural grandstand or stadium. From there, spectators might watch in safety. Telescopes and binoculars were provided for those who wished to observe the slaughter of men and animals at closer range. They expected a grand show, a martial display. Those who came too early rented rooms for the night in Fairfax Court House or Centerville.

Among the watching crowds were some professionals: newspaper reporters, artists, and illustrators. Abraham Lincoln was not there. He was at the Executive Mansion in Washington waiting for news.

Jefferson Davis, President of the Confederacy, was not there either, but he was on the way. He could not endure the strain of the silent hours in Richmond. Calling for his bodyguard, he rode toward Manassas.

CHRONOLOGY 1

APRIL 12, 1861. Confederate General Pierre Gustave Toutant Beauregard attacks Fort Sumter, the Federal garrison on an island off the coast of South Carolina.

APRIL 13. The fort surrenders to the Rebels. The American Civil War begins.

APRIL 15. President Abraham Lincoln calls for all loyal states to send volunteers to Washington to "put down the rebellion." The response is immediate. At the same time, the Southern build-up commences; recruits pour into Richmond to aid the Confederacy.

JUNE 10. In the first action of the war, Colonel John B. Magruder of the Confederacy defeats a small Union force at Fort Bethel, Virginia.

While the 90-day recruits drill in the streets of Washington, a Confederate force of 20,000 men under Beauregard digs in at Manassas Junction, thirty miles away. From this strategic spot, where the Manassas Gap and Orange and Alexandria Railroad lines meet, Beauregard can move to stop any Union advance on Richmond. His camp also poses an immediate threat to Washington.

In a series of fiery editorials, Horace Greeley, editor of the New York *Daily Tribune*, urges that Union troops take Richmond before July 20, the date set for the meeting of the Rebel Congress.

JUNE 29. Lincoln calls a Cabinet meeting to determine the best plan for expelling Beauregard from Manassas. Union General Irvin I. McDowell's suggestion of a three-column strike against the Junction is finally approved.

JULY 9. Aware that the first batch of recruits will soon be released from active service, Lincoln informs McDowell that he must be ready to march on Manassas within a week.

JULY 16. McDowell's march to Manassas begins. Thirty-five thousand Union troops leave Washington amid cheering crowds.

Fifty miles northwest of Manassas, at the entrance to the Shenandoah Valley, 9,000 Confederate troops under the command of General Joseph E. Johnston have taken up positions. Beauregard is counting on these men for support in the battle to come. Nine miles north of Johnston, Union General Robert Patterson commands 18,000 troops. His orders are to move south and engage Johnston's men, but he stalls.

On July 17, fearful of the local Rebels, and irked by the fact that McDowell, twenty-nine years his junior, is superior in command, Patterson decides not to engage Johnston, and withdraws his forces.

JULY 18. At 1:00 A.M. Johnston is ordered by Confederate President Jefferson Davis to join Beauregard.

Throughout the day, the Union troops, tired and discouraged, straggle into Centerville, north of the Confederate encampment. A Union division of more than 1,000 men is sent to Blackburn's Ford, across the river called Bull Run, to obtain information about the depth of the water, obstacles, and so on. Forgetting that the ford will be guarded, the Yankees blunder down the east bank within range of Rebel sharpshooters on the opposite side—only to scramble back under a hail of enemy rifle and artillery fire. A number of Union men are killed or wounded.

After this initial action, Beauregard meets with his generals to draw up a battle plan: he will launch a surprise flank attack against McDowell's troops before they have recovered from their exhausting march. The plan—modeled on Napoleon's Austerlitz strategy—is to throw the Yankees off balance with a left-wing jab; the right wing will then deliver the main blow, crossing Bull Run and smashing into the left flank of the Union force.

JULY 20. In the evening, McDowell announces a battle plan of his own; it is similar to Beauregard's. He will strike first at Stone Bridge, the Rebels' most heavily fortified spot. His right wing—the main force—will then sweep across Bull Run at Sudley Springs, engaging the Confederate left and advancing to cut off the railroad to the Shenandoah Valley.

Earlier that day, Johnston's troop train arrives at Manassas with the major part of his force. Johnston assumes command of the Confederate Army. He is not in favor of Beauregard's Austerlitz plan, but because of his unfamiliarity with the terrain around Bull Run, he agrees to a compromise. Beauregard will command Confederate troops in the field. The Rebel attack, postponed with Beauregard's consent until the rest of Johnston's men arrive, is finally set for 8:00 Sunday morning, July 21.

On the eve of battle, the Rebels are stretched along the west bank of Bull Run for almost eight miles. Union infantry units harass them with gunfire from the east side of the river. Spectators eager to watch the coming fray crowd into Fairfax Court House and Centerville; for them a holiday mood prevails.

McDowell Strikes First

General McDowell had only one possible advantage in the face of Beauregard's plans for a handsome victory. He could move first. And that is what he did. He struck at the Confederate position at Stone Bridge at six o'clock on Sunday morning, exactly two hours before Beauregard's flanking attack was scheduled.

In the New York *Daily Tribune*, editor Horace Greeley had demanded that the Union Army enter Richmond on the twentieth of July. The Union Army was already one day late, and McDowell seemed determined to make up for those lost hours.

Stone Bridge was the most heavily fortified position in the Rebel lines. The bridge was old and narrow, barely wide

Opposing regiments, from New York and Alabama, in action

enough for two carts abreast. No sane general would attempt to move an army across a single span of stone, but the water was shallow on either side. The Federal infantry could wade across, sweep around behind the Rebel guards, and establish a strong foothold on the west bank. By driving a wedge into the Rebel lines, the little bridge would become an easily protected ramp across the river.

The Union attack started with a heavy cannonade by Ricketts' guns. A spirited rush of blue infantry followed. The men halted just out of rifle range, spread out, and crawled forward under cover of the timber along the east bank. Federal shells swept the Warrenton Turnpike empty from Stone Bridge to Henry House on the hill.

Beauregard was caught by surprise, but he moved swiftly, still bent on launching his Napoleonic attack. He issued a paper shower of orders. Mounted messengers spurred out of Manassas for the line, where they were either misunderstood or ignored.

Johnston's staff officers waited for a confirming order from him. Beauregard's own field commanders, although they had been briefed on the flank attack, either did not understand the written orders or failed to follow them.

The hero of Fort Sumter sat in his headquarters, his eyes half-closed, imagining the swift, wheeling movement of infantry units dashing forward and to the right across Bull Run. But Beauregard's dream of a slashing advance amounted to no more than a few floundering movements through tangled undergrowth.

The soldiers had no clear idea of what they were supposed to do. They were soon ankle-deep in muck, or knocked out of position by bull briers and dense willows. Unable to see clearly through the morning mists, they halted. The company commanders were alarmed. On all sides, men hacked and flopped through the marshy woods. They shouted challenges to each other and threatened to fire on their own comrades. The flank attack failed because it never got started.

Yet the failure of his plan proved to be a blessing in disguise for Beauregard. The troops on the right were neither wasted nor drawn too far from the fighting. Later that day, Beauregard discovered he could use them to strengthen his center line, where the Union demonstration had doubled in strength.

While the guns still battered at Stone Bridge, McDowell's troops jabbed at Blackburn's Ford, site of the first action on July 18. Like the demonstration at Stone Bridge, this attack was launched with some spirit and a great deal of noise. The blue infantry concealed themselves along the bank and fired steadily across Bull Run.

The purpose of the double attack was to divert attention and artillery fire away from the Union right wing, where the major attack would be launched. The ruse worked as well as McDowell could have hoped. In less than two hours, the Confederate Army was on the defensive, with the center of its lines fighting hard.

McDowell Presses Forward

The first lesson of Bull Run, namely that it is both easier and wiser to use untrained troops for defense than offense, was soon demonstrated. There is something very comforting about a large tree. Given plenty of ammunition and steady, calm encouragement, the rawest recruit will defend the piece of ground before him. A company of volunteers on the defensive behind stones, dirt heaps, and fallen trees suddenly becomes as strong as a hundred men with iron fangs and claws. It was now up to McDowell's untrained and untried soldiers to break the stiffened Rebel lines.

The Union general drew on his white cotton gloves, a trade-mark by which he was known, and swung up on his horse. His observers reported that Beauregard had shifted his reserves to the center, an obvious move. It was not possible to tell at once whether an assault was only a feint or the real thing.

Besides, whatever the battle plan, a few hotheads sensing a chance for glory could change a feint into an all-out attack. One man had only to pick up the battle standard and run forward. For most of the men in both armies, that was the field maneuver they understood best: follow the flag.

McDowell led the flank attack himself, according to plan. He rode out at the head of his right wing, made up of 18,000 infantry, cavalry, and artillery soldiers with their horses and reserve troops. This powerful force was to loop three miles upstream to a place called Sudley Springs Ford. The sun was

McDowell's infantry advances upstream toward Sudley Springs

up, and the men were in good spirits. When the sullen murmur of the cannon faded, they could hear the church bells ringing at Centerville and Fairfax Court House. It was going to be a beautiful Sunday, hot and dry, with just a slight breeze blowing.

The action was too hot in the center of the Rebel lines for the men to hear church bells. With Johnston's approval, Beauregard sent the infantry of Ewell, Jones, and "Dutch" Longstreet trotting forward through the fields and woods to repel a possible full-scale attack.

There was still no news from the rest of Johnston's army. General Kirby-Smith and Colonel Jubal Early were on their way, the men loaded on two trains, but no one knew when they would arrive. Beauregard exchanged worried glances with his superior. Johnston stared at a map and dropped his finger at a red spot labeled Matthews House, a small wooden dwelling on the crest of a hill north of Stone Bridge. It would be a good idea to reinforce that spot until the Union Army revealed the point of its main attack.

Any man in reasonably good health and unburdened by heavy gear can walk at the rate of four miles per hour. But McDowell knew that his green troops could never reach Sudley Springs Ford in so short a time. The men were ignorant of war. They would halt or scatter each time a Rebel cannon ball came whuffling across the sky. Worse, it was soon discovered that the maps were inaccurate. There were unexpected turns, twists, forks, and crossroads along the way.

Only the regulars, some infantry, and Ricketts' artillery had wits enough to stand still when they lost their way. With veteran know-how, they dragged their equipment off to one side and waited until someone appeared to direct them.

Other units, only half-trained, became quickly disorganized. They marched boldly down the narrow paths to somebody's pigpen, and then came milling back to the road, out of position. Others grew bored with waiting while maps were studied, and struck out across country. They got lost looking for short cuts to the ford. Men became separated from their officers. Orders went astray. Units milled about and stepped on one another's toes.

In spite of the tangle and confusion of men and orders, the maneuver was made. However, it took four hours instead of one to get the Union right wing into position near Sudley Springs Ford. This was no lightning stroke to send the Rebels reeling back to Richmond. Rather, the Union Army had made a sluggish shift. The straggling columns scrambled through the shallows at the ford. Hot and weary, they heaved the gun carriages across, then climbed up the west bank. The men squeezed water from their trousers, emptied their boots, and wrung out their socks. The cavalry came boiling across the ford, and the infantry scattered to let them pass.

High Noon

The rallying point was Sudley Church, a low, rickety building in need of a fresh coat of paint. There were no regular services at Sudley Church on July 21, 1861. General McDowell had arrived to deliver a different sermon—expressed in shellfire, smoke, and steel. But the Union Army was not ready to attack.

The sun was high. It was getting on toward noon. The men cheerfully ignored the fact that they had been scheduled to arrive three hours earlier. It was cool beneath the trees around the church, and the men had been awake since long before dawn. There was water to drink and hardtack to

Sudley Church, the rallying point for McDowell's major attack

munch, that fried ration which tasted as though made of equal parts of crackers and cement. The men wanted to rest and eat.

McDowell shrugged off the delay and dispatched pickets. He spread out his men east and west in position to attack. Sherman's brigade had been left to cross another ford and anchor the east end of the line at Bull Run. The solid mass of men would drive south from the church to the Warrenton Turnpike. In McDowell's plan, the Confederate left wing would be rolled up like so much tattered gray carpet.

Meanwhile, fond memories of the chalky classrooms of West Point and the textbook battle of Austerlitz had faded from the mind of General Beauregard. The Rebels hammered at Stone Bridge and Blackburn's Ford. When riders reported little or no action south of Stone Bridge, Beauregard knew that McDowell's main force must have moved north. The Rebel reinforcements sent to Matthews House would not be sufficient to check any large Federal attack on the left.

Beauregard and Johnston began to shift their men again. They were almost too late. The Union skirmishers, McDowell's crack infantry, were already on the move. They had picked their way down the bridle paths from the Sudley Church and opened fire on the men sheltered behind the stone walls and weathered sheds of Matthews House farm. A runner went flying to the Rebel rear. He passed General T. J. Jackson's Virginia infantry stationed in and around nearby Henry House, another larger farm.

The soldiers there tried to hear what the runner was shouting to General Bee on horseback. Something about the Yankees getting close.

Bee flung out his arm and ordered his men to seize and hold the wooded plateau west of Henry House Hill. The men plunged into the thickets and began throwing up flimsy barricades.

Artillery Cover

Artillery support for McDowell's main attack was already under way. Ricketts' Yankee drivers uncoiled their long whips and snaked them out to crack and pop over the straining horses. The animals lunged into the harness. Their hoofs sank deep into the soft ground. The wooden brakes on the off-wheels smoked as gun carriages were turned until the muzzles pointed toward Henry House and the woods to the west.

Even before the horses were unhitched and led to the rear, the loaders snatched out powder bags and started to stack solid shot and the lighter, fused shells.

Shouts and commands rang up and down the line as the two batteries made ready. The powder bags were split and

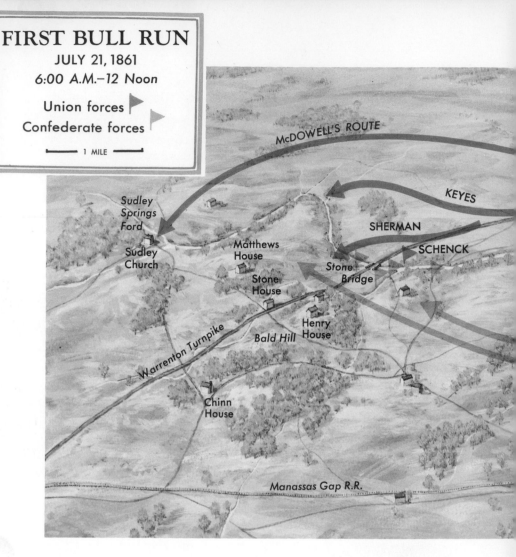

McDOWELL'S ROUTE

KEYES

Sudley
Springs
Ford

SHERMAN

SCHENCK

Sudley
Church

Matthews
House

Stone
Bridge

Stone
House

Henry
House

Warrenton Turnpike

Bald Hill

Chinn
House

Manassas Gap R.R.

crammed into the muzzles of the eight guns. Shell fuses were measured and trimmed. Safely rammed home, the shells would be ignited by the discharge of each cannon. The gun muzzles were raised and trained.

Another shout and the eight cannons bucked and blasted. The gunners scampered like demons to swab the iron gullets cool for the next loading. The shells whined away, hissing like sky snakes. They crashed in scarlet bursts among the trees where General Bee's Rebels were hidden. The cannon

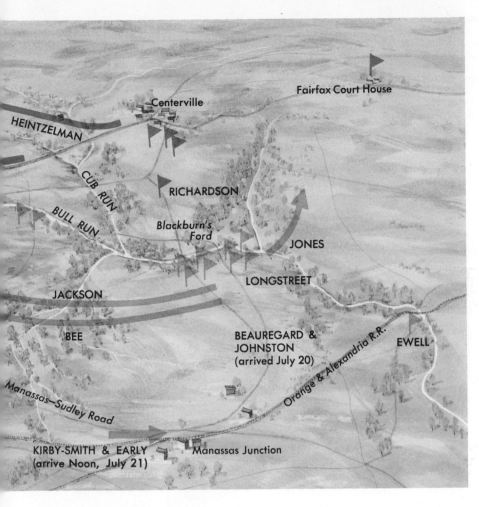

Fairfax Court House

Centerville

HEINTZELMAN

CUB RUN

BULL RUN

RICHARDSON

Blackburn's Ford

JONES

LONGSTREET

JACKSON

BEE

BEAUREGARD & JOHNSTON (arrived July 20)

Orange & Alexandria R.R.

EWELL

Manassas–Sudley Road

KIRBY-SMITH & EARLY (arrive Noon, July 21)

Manassas Junction

roared and bucked in recoil, while the gun crews toiled to service their killing-engines.

Henry House was hit again and again by shells and solid shot. Chimney bricks, bits of boards, flying spears of glass came sailing out of the smoke and dust. The Rebels piled out of the shattered house and sprinted for the woods.

The cannon fire swept west along the Warrenton Turnpike. Fountains of earth and broken fence posts bloomed like trees of death in the hot, dry fields. A shell cracked above the turnpike and flung dead men in the dust. One shell fragment struck eighty-four-year-old Judith Henry as she lay on her bed. She died instantly.

General Jackson moved his men forward slightly, the better to support General Bee's troops to his left. Then he just sat there on his horse, with his hands folded on the saddle pommel. He could hear and see the bitter action around Matthews House. He knew now that the main Union attack was headed for the turnpike. His Virginians would be hit and hit hard.

It was nearly two o'clock in the afternoon. The battle had at last been joined.

The Fighting Begins

The Union bugles sounded high and clear. The color-bearers unfurled their regimental battle flags. The Federal infantry—regulars and volunteers—lurched to their feet. Some paused to fix their bayonets with trembling hands before they swept forward after the bright banners.

Yankee artillery (Brady photograph taken after First Bull Run)

To cover their advance, shells and solid shot fizzed overhead and dropped on the tree-covered plateau where Bee's gray infantry lay waiting. The Union troops emerged from the woods in blue clumps, fanned out into long lines, and then trotted forward.

As the blue battalions advanced up the grassy slope, they could identify three houses on the hill. To the left was Matthews House, dimly seen through the smoke and dust. Crouching blue figures moved through its yards and gardens, kneeling to fire, then scrambling forward. Beyond that house and closer to the top of the hill was a stone building, center of the Rebel resistance. It was out of rifle range for the main body of Union troops headed for the turnpike. The third and last house on the hill was Henry House, partly hidden by trees.

The Union color-bearers trotted steadily forward. One was hit. Another man caught the staff before the flag touched the ground. The pace slowed as the slope steepened. Now most of the men were no longer running, but walking swiftly, their faces set. They felt terribly fragile, the men of the front ranks. Musket balls made an odd *thuck* as they drilled the earth before the Union soldiers. There was absolutely nothing to hide behind—only the grass, knee-deep and dry, ready for mowing.

Henry House loomed as big as a castle and as distant as a baron's stronghold on the Rhine. They would never get there —at least not alive. A number of the men turned and broke for the rear. They did not go far. A second wave of infantry a dozen paces back caught up with them. There were blue lines behind that line, too, and still more men pouring out of the woods.

The two batteries of cannon were hitched and dragged forward. The fields north of the Warrenton Turnpike seemed very crowded, and everyone was moving up Henry House Hill. The fleeing men were halted, jostled, and turned back by the waves of men who followed. Thrust into line by red-faced, shouting officers, they stumbled back up the slope.

Bee's Rebel troops waited behind their trees and stones and little walls of earth. They blinked and swallowed. Their throats were dry. There they were! The Yankees! Thousands of them, with bayonets and baggy red breeches and blue jackets, their colors tilting and bobbing along the lines. At command, the Rebels opened fire. The Union front rank thinned as man after man went down.

The Yankees wavered and came on again, to be slugged sprawling in the bloody grass. The next line pressed forward, the soldiers skirting the tumbled bodies. The raw volunteers turned away their eyes from the horrible sight. Their officers called for a volley, but the firing was scattered. While they paused to load, a third wave rushed forward.

The slope was climbed now. The woods were close and straight ahead. A shell smashed Henry House. A window blind sailed through the air, spraying bits of wood. The cannon had been dragged close enough to destroy the house and anyone foolish enough to seek shelter there.

The Union battery fired again, this time to still better effect. The heavy lead balls poured like sleet into the trees and bushes. The men fired at the smoke puffs that drifted between the shell-torn trees. In response, the Rebel volley was sputtering and weaker.

Blue soldiers and gray soldiers fired blindly along the forest fringe. Wild spatters of lead mingled with the deafening racket of smacking rifles and buzzing bullets. The first Yankee soldiers dashed into the woods and were swallowed in the smoke. Flung back out on the grass, they rushed in again, yelling like maniacs. One squad, then another, then a whole company fell upon Bee's defenders.

There came a time when even the thickest, largest, safest tree no longer seemed precious beyond price. That instant occurred when twenty gasping men in blue plunged through the low growth only a dozen paces away. They were led by a hatless young officer with a pistol in one fist, a naked saber in the other. To Bee's troops, these men in blue with their long bright bayonets seemed huge and overpowering. They found their own trees very quickly. Where there had been twenty men in front of them, there were now fifty. It was time to find a thicker, safer tree, a larger rock, a higher mound of earth.

Bee's Confederates grappled gamely, but they were badly mauled. They left their dead and dying and fell back, firing

Bayonets held high, the Union forces launch their main attack

at the blue swarms that darted from tree to tree. Federal cannon had been hauled up to point-blank range and loaded with canister and grapeshot. When a gun roared now, fifty lead balls spewed out of the muzzle. The effect was shattering. The Rebels abandoned the woods and spilled back around Henry House and out onto the turnpike.

The Rebel Line Breaks

The men in blue began to shout—hoarsely at first, then with shrill excitement. They were winning! The Rebel defenses at Stone House were taken in one bloody rush. The infantry smashed through the woods and swung southwest toward the turnpike. A long row of white puffs, like cotton bolls, bloomed along the road.

Even while the Rebels gave ground in confusion, they

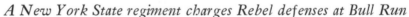

A New York State regiment charges Rebel defenses at Bull Run

struck back hard enough to check the Union advance for a few precious moments. The Federals flopped in the grass and returned the fire. They bit cartridges. They whanged their ramrods, primed, and fired. The roadway was going to be just like the woods. The Rebels would fight fiercely until they were driven off.

The turnpike was bare, just a level stretch of dirt road pocked with shell holes. The Confederates were sprawled along the far shoulder. In a matter of moments, it became a broad dirt goal line to be crossed. Forward went the Union colors again. It was impossible to hear any orders given, but it wasn't necessary to hear. The battle flags headed straight for the turnpike. The Union soldiers loaded, primed, and followed.

Back on the banks of Bull Run, Colonel Sherman stood in his stirrups and bawled for his brigade to cross over. The men pounded down the slope into the water. Bullets splashed all around them. Men shrieked and sagged into the muddy river. Sherman's horse staggered and slipped, soaking the red-haired rider. His men kept on going. They made the far bank and went crashing and shouting through the willows toward Stone House.

Up on the crest, the blue tide had washed over the Warrenton Turnpike and into the meadows beyond. For men who had not, for the most part, ever fought in battle before, the Union soldiers were doing a great deal better than anyone had a right to expect. They rammed forward, scattering Bee's Rebels.

General McDowell cuffed the dust from his spotless white gloves and sent his staff officers to cheer the support troops on. They were winning. They had won, really! Or so they thought.

Ricketts' regular batteries that had done such deadly work at the wooded plateau were dragged up near the top of Henry House Hill. Every second now a dozen lead balls whacked into the shattered building. The flood of blue soldiers continued to surge forward. Their battle flags jerked and tossed through the smoke and dust. As the Confederates fled, the men turned to kneel and fire at the running figures that seemed about to overwhelm them. The Rebel line west of Henry House, mainly Bee's battered troops, had broken. Ricketts' gunners blew on their glowing matches and sighted their next target. The guns slammed and bucked, spraying grapeshot at Jackson's Virginians.

In the meadow south of the turnpike, Beauregard and his officers were striving frantically to prevent a rout. Those desperate moments were recalled by the Southern field commander in his report filed at Richmond after the battle:

"General Johnston and I now set out at full speed for the point of conflict. We arrived there just as Brigadier General Bee's troops, after giving way, were flying in disorder. . . . Every segment of the line we succeeded in forming was again dissolved while another was being formed; more than two thousand men were shouting each some suggestion to his neighbor, their voices mingling with the noise of the shells hurtling overhead, and all word of command drowned in the confusion and uproar."

Jackson Earns a Nickname

Then came one of the moments in time, in the instant of battle action, that men remember and retell for generations. The Union attack was carrying all before it—except at Henry House Hill. There, in spite of the brutal guns of the Federal

Henry House, where Jackson's brigade stopped the Union assault

batteries, the Virginia brigade stood fast, as though their boots had been nailed to the earth. They fired at will, unyielding, ripping at the blue assault that flowed toward them.

General Bee, trying to rally his troops, saw how calmly T. J. Jackson guided his men, seated on his horse, with his hands still folded on the saddle pommel. Bee swung his own mount out across the meadow, brandished his sword, and bellowed: "There is Jackson standing like a stone wall! Rally behind the Virginians!" Then Bee fell, shot dead.

Beauregard heard the shout through the din of bullets. He turned to stare. The shattered Rebel units heard Bee's dying call to them. Like Beauregard, they turned to look.

A stone wall? Where? Any man who stood fast under the murderous fire of rifles, muskets, and cannon shells must be either a fool or a hero. Like a stone wall? Impossible. Yet it was true.

The battle flag of Jackson's Virginia brigade rippled over the billowing smoke. The men stood in even ranks, their dead and wounded comrades tumbled at their feet. Their return fire stuttered, banged, and rattled. They worked their weapons until their hands blistered, but they never stopped firing. Not a man moved to the rear. The Union cannon fire halted for a moment, and a blue unit stood exposed. The Virginians flung up their rifles and slashed their attackers into bleeding knots of dusty blue. It was a fateful moment.

The Union Line Breaks

The impetus of the Union attack was lost. The forward line broke. Some men dropped in the ditch or fell out on the highway. The rest rushed back toward the shelter of the smashed and ruined Henry House. This time there was no second or third rank to catch and hold the fleeing men. The ground before Jackson's Virginians began to clear. Groups of Yankees darted off right and left, but none stood strong enough to volley back at the Confederate brigade.

Somehow, through the howl of shells and the excited shouts of men, Beauregard made himself heard. He knew that he must seize this moment that Jackson and his brigade had made. He ordered all the Rebel color-bearers he could find to move forward forty paces. General Bee's broken troops rallied as they saw their flags tilt back toward the turnpike.

General Johnston, riding not far from Beauregard, came across a fresh-looking Rebel regiment. Why weren't they fighting? Who were they, anyway? They were the 4th Alabama; no one had given them any orders. Johnston stabbed his left hand toward Henry House. The Alabama

infantry broke ranks and ran forward to plug the dangerous
gap on Jackson's left. They opened fire and cut down the
blue skirmishers brave enough to crawl out on the turnpike
to rescue the wounded men left moaning in the dust.

Now two Rebel units stood fast on Henry House Hill. The
stone wall was growing.

Meanwhile, at Manassas Junction, a gasping locomotive
shuddered to a halt on the freight siding. Down the long
train, the gray soldiers dropped from the open doorways of
the freight cars and pulled open their cartridge boxes. The
battle banged and roared over the hills to the east. Kirby-
Smith and Jubal Early had arrived with their troops.

General Kirby-Smith herded his men along the back fringe
of the battlefield and then flung them forward to the left of
the 4th Alabama. The stone wall now had important reinforcements.

Jubal Early's fighters formed into companies as rapidly as
they tumbled down into the cinders from the freight cars.
At double time, Early hurried them along the narrow road
that ran past Chinn House, at a southwest angle to the Warrenton Turnpike. Kirby-Smith's men covered Bald Hill,
their left wing touching Early's right. They stormed forward
together, the cheers of Bee's battered brigade in their ears.

Now the two Union batteries on Henry House Hill were
in trouble. Their infantry support had dwindled and disappeared, looking for cover, after their disastrous encounter
with Jackson's brigade. The gunners continued to fire when-
ever the dust and smoke thinned enough to let them see the
enemy. The cannon were out of range for most of the
Confederate small arms. Only the Springfield rifles seized at
Harpers Ferry arsenal could be set for distances greater than
five hundred yards. The artillerymen cursed and went back

to their deadly work. That was the infantry for you, they thought. Just when you needed them most, they disappeared.

A Fatal Surprise

The gunners were not given much time to worry about the infantry. Out of the roaring swirl of dust and din and dying, a small group of Confederates launched a counter-attack across the turnpike. Beauregard had noticed them before the battle. They were a militia group, of course, outfitted by their state . . . in blue uniforms!

These soldiers in blue came in a pack, streaming across the road, shrieking their yell of triumph. Their bayonets glittered. The Union gun crews saw them coming and jumped to the conclusion that a flank attack must have pushed Jackson's brigade back into the meadow. The gunners waved

A Brady photograph of Zouaves who fought in the Civil War

their powder-blackened arms and shouted encouragement.

The blue-clad Rebels paused and aimed their steel-pronged rifles. The gunners gasped in horror as the volley caught them unawares, ripping into them at deadly close range. They screamed that they were Ricketts' men. They yelled their unit number. They could not believe that the soldiers in blue were actually the enemy. There must be some mistake.

There was a sudden, short lull. Then the order to charge was given in the soft drawl of a Southerner. There was no mistake about it. The wicked bayonets and smashing pistols exploded through the dust in a fatal surprise. Ricketts' bleeding gunners huddled numbly behind their cannon, clutching their useless swabs and rammers. The professionals were torn to death by amateurs in wrong-colored uniforms.

The Union attack, so bravely carried so close to success, collapsed all at once. Ricketts' guns had been taken. The yards around Henry House were nearly empty. Long gray lines of Confederates stretched solid from Stone Bridge to Chinn House Road. The reinforcements had come just in time. The blue fighters hung on grimly, but their strength was spent. Rebel cavalry stabbed through the gray lines, scattering the Union infantry every time they re-formed.

Now the Confederate defenders shifted to sporadic counterattacks up and down the line. The two armies stood toe to toe for an hour, hammering and slugging, spilling more blood into the dust. But the blue tide had been checked by the gray stone wall and began to ebb. The victory went to the Confederates: hard-fought, well-earned, and high in price.

On Henry House Hill, the ex-professor of military tactics and ex-minister of God sat calmly on his horse, calling encouragement to his company commanders. Brigadier General T. J. Jackson had a new nickname: "Stonewall."

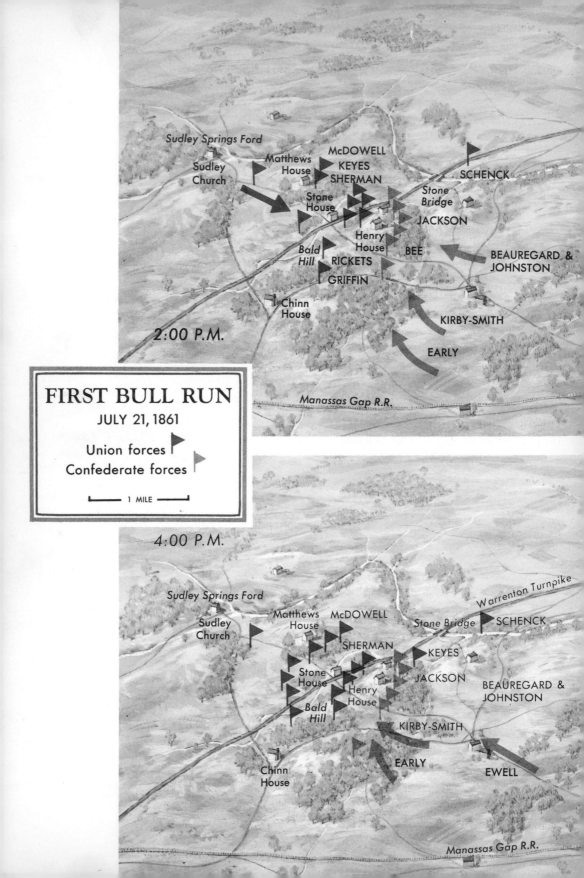

2:00 P.M.

Sudley Springs Ford
Sudley Church
Matthews House
McDOWELL
KEYES
SHERMAN
SCHENCK
Stone House
Stone Bridge
JACKSON
Henry House
BEE
Bald Hill
RICKETS
BEAUREGARD & JOHNSTON
GRIFFIN
Chinn House
KIRBY-SMITH
EARLY
Manassas Gap R.R.

FIRST BULL RUN

JULY 21, 1861

Union forces
Confederate forces

1 MILE

4:00 P.M.

Sudley Springs Ford
Sudley Church
Matthews House
McDOWELL
Warrenton Turnpike
Stone Bridge
SCHENCK
SHERMAN
KEYES
Stone House
JACKSON
Henry House
BEAUREGARD & JOHNSTON
Bald Hill
KIRBY-SMITH
Chinn House
EARLY
EWELL
Manassas Gap R.R.

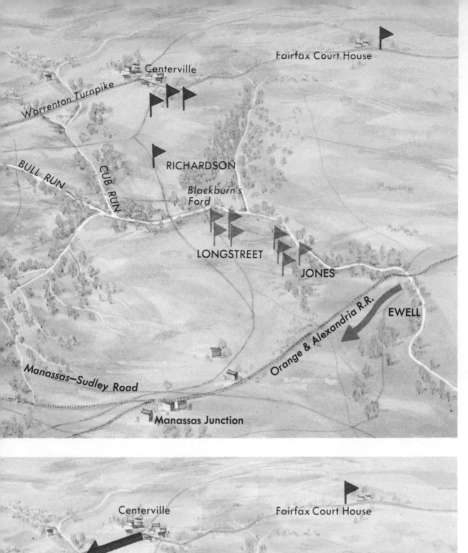

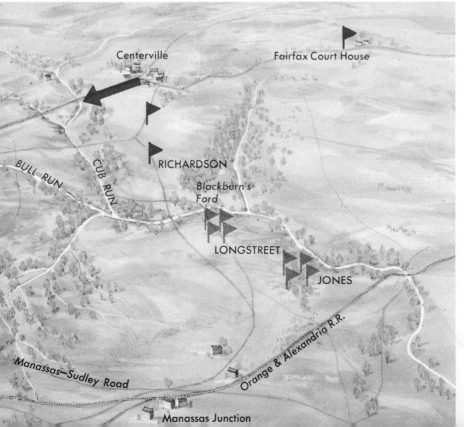

CHRONOLOGY II

JULY 21, 6:00 A.M.—11:30 A.M.   The Union force opens fire at Stone Bridge, taking the Rebels by surprise. Beauregard immediately commands his men to launch the flank attack toward Centerville, but his ill-trained troops, groping through heavy morning mists and impeding undergrowth, make no decisive advance.

A second Union attack at Blackburn's Ford diverts Rebel fire from McDowell's right wing—18,000 infantry, cavalry, and artillery soldiers—which is proceeding from Centerville toward Sudley Springs. At the head of the right wing rides McDowell himself.

11:30 A.M.—12:00 NOON.   The Union right wing straggles across Sudley Springs Ford in disorganized groups. The crossing is three hours behind schedule. As McDowell advances, Confederate troops in the vicinity fall back to Henry House Hill, south of the Warrenton Turnpike.

12:00 NOON—1:00 P.M.   McDowell's force reaches Sudley Church, halts to eat, and forms for attack. The troops will drive south from the church toward the turnpike.

1:00 P.M.—2:00 P.M.   Messengers warn Beauregard that McDowell's main force is at his extreme left. Even as Beauregard begins to shift the bulk of his troops to meet the expected attack, Union skirmishers advance down the bridle path from Sudley Church and make contact with Rebels around Matthews House.

In the woods west of Henry House, Confederate General Barnard E. Bee's troops are battered by Union cannons.

2:00 P.M.—3:00 P.M.   McDowell launches his main assault. His battalions pour from the woods, fanning out and advancing steadily up the grassy slope toward Henry House Hill. From their position south of the turnpike, Bee's infantry troops open fire on the Union men, hoping to stem the flood. But McDowell's men press on.

Unable to withstand the brutal Yankee fire, Bee's forces and the other Rebel troops west of Henry House are driven onto a section of the turnpike to the north.

Captain James Ricketts' and Captain Charles Griffin's Union batteries push on toward Henry House, while other Union forces storm the Rebel defenses at Stone House, forcing Confederates there to abandon their positions. The blue tide then swings southwest, carrying the fighting over the turnpike and into the meadows beyond.

As the Union attack gains strength, Johnston and Beauregard rush to the meadows in a desperate attempt to rally their scattered troops.

On Henry House Hill, however, the Yankees are held at bay by Confederate General T. J. Jackson's Virginia Brigade, which stands "like a stone wall" against Union rifles, muskets, and cannons. Bee, trying to re-form his troops, sees this amazing sight and yells, "Rally behind the Virginians!" The next instant he is killed by a Yankee bullet. As the Yankees begin to fall back under the Virginians' deadly rifle fire, Beauregard seizes his chance and commands Confederate color-bearers to advance forty paces. Bee's troops, revitalized, rush forward to support Jackson.

3:00 P.M.–4:30 P.M. Confederate reinforcements under General Edmund Kirby-Smith and Colonel Jubal Early arrive at the scene of the action and advance toward Bald Hill.

Members of a Confederate militia unit dressed in blue uniforms dash toward Ricketts' positions on Henry House Hill. Thinking these men are reinforcements, the Yankees hold their cannon fire until it is too late. The stunned Union men are decimated.

The Confederates counterattack across the turnpike, regaining positions held earlier. The Union forces are now on the defensive all along the line.

4:30 P.M. TO SUNDOWN. McDowell orders his troops to retreat via Stone Bridge and Sudley Springs to Centerville, where he has 10,000 men in reserve. Spectators on the hills east of the battlefield are terrified at the sight of the bloody, battle-worn Union soldiers fleeing in defeat. The onlookers stampede, knocking over picnic baskets and leaving their food and possessions behind; the retreat turns into a disorganized rout.

To add to the confusion, a horse and wagon is overturned at a small bridge over Cub Run, blocking the road. The panicked crowd pours around the obstacle, crying, "The Rebel cavalry is coming!" Beauregard, however, has no intention of pursuing the Union Army, and it escapes.

JULY 22. The demoralized Yankee troops lumber across the Long Bridge over the Potomac and into Washington. At Bull Run, the Confederates clean the battlefield of loot and bury their dead.

Almost 5,000 men have been lost in the battle; Union losses are 2,896 killed and wounded to the Confederates' 1,982. July 21, 1861 comes to be called Abraham Lincoln's "crucifixion day"—years of strife lie ahead for the American Nation.

The Outcome

Just at sundown, when Kirby-Smith's men and Early's troops smashed back across the Warrenton Turnpike, McDowell knew that the battle was lost for that day. He passed the order for the army to retreat to Centerville, five miles nearer Washington. At Centerville, he had left nearly 10,000 men in reserve.

There would be a time for more fighting, but not at Henry House and not along the turnpike. After this long day's battle, the Federal infantry was outnumbered, cut up by Rebel cavalry, and had lost their best artillery support. They had been beaten. It was time to retreat, to get off the field before they were surrounded and captured.

A retreat is not a rout, not a running away. In military terms, a retreat is an orderly withdrawal of men from a position they cannot defend without running risk of being destroyed altogether. Ideally, the troops move toward their center and form into columns. Then they simply march back to some previously selected position in the rear. Disciplined troops may do this even under heavy fire.

At Bull Run, the green troops of Irvin McDowell turned a retreat into a rout because they had not had enough drill in the maneuver of retreat. It was not because the men had lost their nerve and refused to fight. Part of the blame fell on McDowell himself—more than was his share. This happened because he had neglected to establish rear positions in case retreat became necessary. The men were ordered back with no clear idea where they should go.

Lieutenant Josiah Favill of the 57th New York Infantry

told how an orderly retreat may turn into a terrified flight. What the men saw about them, or what they didn't see, was of prime importance to each man and to the army as a whole. Not long afterward, he described what happened when the Confederates shifted from defense to attack at sunset:

"As the long line came nearer and nearer, our Colonel Martin ordered us all to fall in, and with muskets in hand, we stood, simply watching the gradual approach of this overwhelming force, and the disappearance of our troops . . . now there was nobody left, and our colonel ordered us to countermarch to the rear . . . as we continued going to the rear and saw no fresh dispositions [of Union troops] we came to the conclusion that we were running away . . . presently we came up with the rear of the troops that had preceded us into battle, but looked in vain for new defensive dispositions.

"Everywhere was hurry and confusion, the wagons and batteries filled the roads, while the men spread out on either side, gradually losing their formations and fast becoming reckless. There was no rear guard, nor any arrangements for holding the enemy in check, and if they really had appeared, they might have captured us all without difficulty.

"Now everyone was anxious to be first, and so by degree, the men of various regiments got mixed up together, and thus, finding themselves without officers, accelerated their steps until at last it became a precipitate flight to the rear."

Although Lieutenant Favill did not see them, a battalion of regular infantry moved alone up Henry House Hill and fought a hard, harassing action with the Rebels who had recovered their old positions on the plateau. In spite of brave work there and elsewhere, the fact was that the retreat to Centerville had turned into a rout.

Flight

The panic did not begin at once—not until the main body of the Union Army had splashed back through the muddy waters of Bull Run. The disgrace was later thrown at General McDowell, and never again was he to lead a Union army in battle. The real fault lay with the hundreds of spectators who had lounged and lunched on the eastern edge of the battleground. It had been a holiday for them, just a Sunday excursion, to watch the battle from a safe distance. They had gotten a thrill from the grumble and boom of artillery, without thinking of the men who were torn with bullets, shells, and bayonets in the fields below.

When the army headed back toward Centerville in disordered flight, the spectators were alarmed for their own safety. Picnic hampers were kicked over. Food and wine were carelessly left behind. Rich cigars were thrown away with a curse. Men, women, and children came running down from the slopes, in sudden terror. Even senators and congressmen joined the crowds of civilians who plunged out onto the same highway that the army was using. Women and girls screamed at the sight of Wisconsin soldiers in bloody gray jackets. They feared these men were Rebel raiders who would capture or harm them.

Bull Run had been the largest battle fought on American soil up to that time. It ended in the largest traffic jam on American soil up to that time. One of the senators, Lyman Trumbull of Illinois, described the scene to two fellow senators as "the most shameful rout" you can imagine. He said:

"Efforts were made to rally the men by civilians and others on their way to Centerville, but all to no purpose. Literally, three could have chased 10,000.

"All this stampede was occasioned, as I understand, by a charge of not exceeding 200 cavalry upon Schenck's column down in the woods, which, instead of repulsing as they could easily have done . . . broke and ran, communicating the panic to everybody they met . . . I suppose 2,000 soldiers came rushing into Centerville in this disorganized condition. At Centerville there was a reserve of 8,000 or 10,000 men under Colonel Miles who had not been in the action, and they were formed in line of battle when we left there, but the enemy did not . . . advance to that point.

"Not very many baggage wagons, perhaps not more than 50, were advanced beyond Centerville. From them the horses were mostly unhitched and the wagons left standing in the road when the stampede took place. . . . Thousands of shovels were thrown out upon the road, also axes, boxes of

Terror and confusion reign on the little bridge over Cub Run

provisions, etc. In some instances, wagons were upset to get them out of the road, and the road was full of four-horse wagons retreating as fast as possible, and also full of flying soldiers who could not be made to stop at Centerville . . . I am dreadfully disappointed and mortified."

The Senator was mortified, but most of the vast mob was simply frightened. Some unknown Confederate gunner sent a shell whistling across the sky. The shell happened to strike squarely a wagon and horses in the middle of a small bridge over Cub Run. This completed the chaos. The road to Washington was now blocked.

Panic

Five minutes after that single shell burst on the little bridge over the knee-deep creek, terror swept through the mass of soldiers and civilians. Bits and pieces of the disorganized army crammed past. They pushed over and around the jam of wheeled vehicles packed with white-faced women and roaring men. Every new flood of men or horses caused a new wave of panic.

Rumors sprinted faster than the fleetest raw volunteer. The Rebel "Black horse cavalry" was coming! It was there! No, here! It was close, closer! It was right on top of them!

Knots of soldiers punched and struggled to get away. Riderless horses galloped here and there. People were panic-stricken by an enemy that wasn't there. The Rebel cavalry had halted miles back from Cub Run.

The wind shifted during the long twilight, and low, dark rain clouds blew in over the hills and highway. Before darkness closed down completely, chaos spread everywhere. Voices babbled of death, capture, prison camps. An army

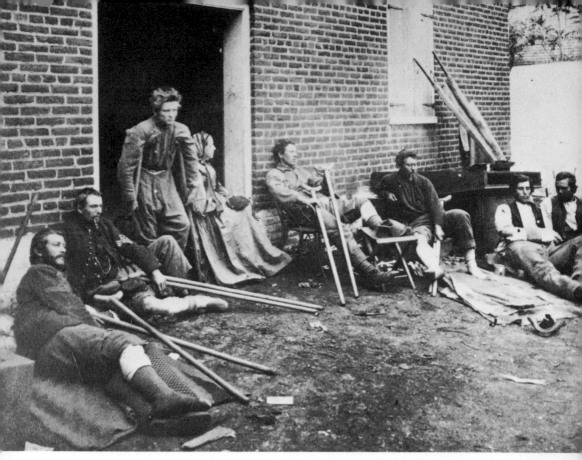

A few of thousands of Americans wounded in the Civil War

had marched out of Washington only five days before. A rabble rushed back in a desperate search for safety. But there was no pursuit.

Trophies of Battle

Just before dark, the President of the Confederacy, Jefferson Davis, arrived with his bodyguard. He expected to find the Rebel force broken by defeat, for that was the tale brought to him by some of General Bee's runaways. Instead, he found Johnston and Beauregard trying to make sense out of the scrawled notes sent in from the field by the brigade commanders—Early, Kirby-Smith, Howard, Longstreet, Jackson, and the rest.

"Stonewall" Jackson, the hero of Henry House Hill, urged an immediate attack on Washington. His was a lonely voice, muttering into his beard that with 50,000 troops he could destroy McDowell's army and overrun the city.

Beauregard was not tempted by Jackson's proposal. He knew that his men were nearly as disorganized by victory as the Union troops were by defeat. As a compromise, he sent out several more squadrons of cavalry to round up and bring in Yankee prisoners. Nearly 600 men were captured; among others a United States congressman, Alfred Ely of New York, frock coat, top hat, and all.

The rest of Beauregard's gray troops strayed across the fields and slopes around the battlefield. They prowled through the shattered pinewoods and tangles. They walked up and down the many dirt roads between the farms. They bragged about the number of Yankees they had killed, although only the Virginia brigade was due great honor.

The Rebels gathered a tremendous quantity of military loot, not even counting the valuable cannon of Ricketts' batteries. The stuff was everywhere, discarded by the Federals in their hasty flight. There were horses with fancy saddles and trappings, loaded wagons and carts, tents, blanket rolls, muskets, and rifles by the thousands, pistols, canteens, sabers, cartridge boxes, belt buckles, and foodstuffs by the crate and barrel.

Up in the eastern hills, they picked up other treasures abandoned by the spectators. They found such luxuries as a woman's scented handkerchief, a gay carriage robe, a basket of ripe pears, picnic hampers still half full of food, a cedar humidor filled with fine cigars.

Before the rain started to fall that night, the Rebels gleaned the harvest of what Colonel Louis Blenker, a German-American from the 8th New York Infantry, called simply "a panic, all at once."

Shocking Losses

Abraham Lincoln was a man of fixed habits. On Sunday afternoons, the President went for his carriage ride. Toward evening on July 21, he returned to the White House, changed his coat, and walked over to army headquarters. There he read this dispatch from McDowell: "The day is lost. Save Washington and the remnants of the army. The routed troops will not re-form."

All through that dark night, in the drenching rain, the soldiers of the Union Army stumbled toward Washington. They were beaten and bedraggled. It rained all day Monday, too, as though the skies wept for the boys left on the battle-field.

The soldiers who returned crossed the Long Bridge over the Potomac with weary steps and staggered down Pennsylvania Avenue. Some pitched their tents on front lawns. Others simply collapsed on doorsteps, so utterly spent that they slept as they fell. The women of the city dragged them indoors and fed them. They washed their uniforms and hung them up to steam and dry.

President Lincoln lay sleepless, his long legs cramped, on the horsehair couch in his Cabinet room. He could hear the trundle of guns and carts. He recognized the exhaustion in the cracked voices of the drivers urging their horses another few blocks to shelter and comfort. The poet Walt Whitman called July 21, 1861, Abraham Lincoln's "crucifixion day."

It seemed to all who had taken part in the First Battle of Bull Run that the casualty lists would be fearful to read. And they were—although not as large as in later battles in the Civil War. A great many men were simply lost. Days passed before an accurate tally could be made.

Officially, the Federals lost 2,896 men. Others would soon die of wounds and disease in the wretched hospitals in and around Washington. Confederate losses were less heavy: 1,982 men killed and wounded. They also would have additional losses from wounds and disease. When the sum total of casualties was added up after the war, the losses from disease were greater than battle casualties.

To both sides, the figures were shocking. These dead men were not Indians or French or British or Mexicans. They were Americans—Yankees and Rebels if you liked—but still Americans. That was what made the figures so shocking. Nearly 5,000 men had been slaughtered in a single afternoon:

The long bridge over the Potomac River, seen from Washington

husbands and sons, brothers and friends. They had come from Boston or Birmingham, Rochester or Richmond, New Haven or New Orleans, Columbia, Charleston, and Madison, Wisconsin. All were Americans.

The fancy uniforms, the banners of bright silk, the blare of military bands could not hide the truth. Out went the telegrams and letters of official sympathy: *"Dear Sir or Madame, It gives me the greatest sorrow to report that . . . killed in action . . . gallant defender of his country's . . . sincerest regrets . . . supreme sacrifice . . . honor and duty . . . the nation mourns with you . . ."*

As the results of Bull Run became known, people realized that the war was not a game. It was not a holiday of heroism, gallant actions, and minor flesh wounds. War was a grim business that mangled and disfigured, crippled and diseased both animals and men. It also wasted and ruined land and houses. The shattered shell of Henry House was only the first dwelling destroyed by cannon fire. Old Judith Henry was only the first innocent civilian to suffer from the destroying blight of war.

This grim business would go on and on. The ninety-day volunteers could go home. They would be replaced by men who signed up for nine months or three years. Later, when those eager volunteers had been exhausted, soldiers would be taken by forced draft into both Southern and Northern armies. The days when a man or boy could choose to fight or stay at home would soon be over.

In any case, all volunteer troops would be merged with the Federal regulars. The custom of electing officers by popular vote was forbidden. Lincoln agreed with his generals that only West Point graduates could provide the discipline that war demanded.

Other harsh measures followed. The blockade of Southern ports by ships of the Union Navy was stepped up. Any ship that could float in the Atlantic would be pressed into service to seal off the Confederate States from Europe. The Confederacy hoped to be recognized by England because of that nation's interest in the cotton crop, which flowed to British textile mills at the rate of a million bales a year. If this should happen, it was important to the Union that the harbors of Charleston, Savannah, and New Orleans be closed by a combination of permanent patrol and the sinking of old hulks in the mouths of Southern harbors.

The United States Congress passed a resolution to define officially the scope and purpose of the war. It was carefully worded so that civilians and soldiers alike would understand that the war was a struggle "to defend and maintain the supremacy of the Constitution, and to preserve the dignity, equality and rights of the several states unimpaired."

With this resolution, the Congress of the North served warning to the Congress of the South. The fighting would continue until the Confederacy was finally defeated and the seceded states brought back into the Union. Lincoln's government refused to accept the Southern dream that America might remain "a house divided against itself."

Bitter Lessons for the Union

The First Battle of Bull Run awoke the North to cold reality. Before the Union could launch another campaign, a real army must be welded together. Military experts must be found and promoted to responsible positions. Recruits must be organized, trained, and outfitted in order to serve with the regular army under steel-stiff West Point discipline.

Abraham Lincoln,
16th President of the United States

Fancy, impractical uniforms, suitable only for the parade ground, must be discarded. The Zouaves, the kilted Highlanders, the Garibaldi Guards would be required to pack away their glittering uniforms, so unsuitable for active campaigns in the field. The textile mills in Massachusetts worked at full speed. Power looms slanted and shuttles flew to weave the sober blue that would uniform Federal soldiers from Taunton to Tennessee.

Bitter lessons had been learned at Bull Run. Wisconsin troops wearing gray uniforms had been fired upon by their own comrades. Ricketts' stalwart gunners, fooled at Henry House by Rebel troops in blue, had been killed and their guns captured. Before long, a Union general, Philip Sheridan, would order any Rebel wearing anything but gray or homespun to be hanged from the nearest tree as a spy.

Union war prisoners captured in the First Battle of Bull Run

The loss of Ricketts' batteries also argued strongly for closer cooperation between infantry and artillery. The men of different units needed to learn the bitter lesson that they were not simply friends fighting on the same piece of ground. For effectiveness and personal safety, several units needed to work together.

Reports of officers like Josiah Favill were read with great attention. The ease with which a retreat turns into a rout was a matter for sober thought. This too must never happen again. Never again the straggling of the march to Manassas. Never again the casual disorder of McDowell's march to Sudley Springs Ford or the flight in terror from imaginary cavalry. Never again!

The bitter lessons of Bull Run were many, but they were not forgotten. Even Colonel Sherman's hot-tempered attacks on newspapermen began to receive attention. Suspected spies were arrested and expelled from Union territory.

Reaction in Richmond

Below the Potomac, the reaction to the Battle of Manassas, as the First Battle of Bull Run was called by the Confederates, was one of general jubilation. Church bells rang out the news of a great victory. The traditional gallantry of the Southern male, the gentleman-warrior, was exalted beyond all reason. Soldiers and civilians alike were convinced by the action at Henry House that any Confederate fighter could whip a dozen Yankees.

To the excited passions of the Southern Rebels, Bull Run seemed a clear proof of Confederate military might. They scoffed at the declaration of the Union Congress and assured one another that total independence for the Confederacy was certain.

The blockade drew more sneers than sighs. Cotton was king. They believed that England and France, too, would recognize the rich lands that grew the "white gold." From Richmond came whispers about plans for iron ships that would smash the Union Navy. The Rebel fleet would keep the ports open to European trade. Ten thousand new Enfield rifles had been ordered from Britain, and designs for mines and torpedoes were on the desk of the Confederate Secretary of the Navy.

Throughout the South, there were glittering receptions for the heroes of Manassas. Any city of size had at least one "Bull Run Ball." Negro musicians played the sweet sentimental strains of "Lorena" and the rousing "Bonny Blue Flag" for their happy, overconfident white masters.

It Will Be a Long War

After Bull Run, the North awoke, while the South dallied
and danced and dreamed. Only the dead men, 5,000 American men and boys, slept, beneath the shot-torn sod between
Manassas Junction and the muddy little river called Bull Run.

All the Confederate half-successes and slow disasters were
still to come. Ahead were the bitter siege of Vicksburg and the
capture of New Orleans that clamped shut the long Mississippi. Ahead were bloody Antietam, the high mark at Ceme-
tery Ridge near Gettysburg, and Sherman's march to the sea

Aftermath of battle at the "muddy little river" called Bull Run

to "make Georgia howl." Ahead was the final stacking of arms at Appomattox Court House. All the weary, half-starved months lay ahead, the cruel years that would grind up precious gold and crush still more precious lives.

Before the war could end, Lincoln would pick over his generals to find a man who could beat Robert E. Lee. He would find him at last, a stumpy, rather silent man who knew how to wage total war: Ulysses S. Grant, "U.S." Grant, whose initials stood for "unconditional surrender."

One week after Bull Run, a Yankee historian, John Motley, peered into the future. He wrote to his wife: "A grim winter is before us. Gather you rosebuds while you may. The war is to be a long one."

FOR FURTHER READING

Nonfiction

ANGLE, PAUL M. and EARL S. MIERS. *The Tragic Years: 1860–1865.* 2 vols. New York: Simon and Schuster, 1960.

BEATIE, RUSSELL H. *Road to Manassas.* New York: Cooper, 1961.

CATTON, BRUCE. *The Coming Fury.* New York: Doubleday, 1961.

———. *Grant Moves South.* Boston: Little, Brown, 1960.

———. *A Stillness at Appomattox.* New York: Doubleday, 1953.

———. *This Hallowed Ground.* New York: Doubleday, 1956.

COMMAGER, HENRY STEELE (Ed.). *The Blue and the Gray.* New York: Bobbs-Merrill, 1950.

DONALD, DAVID. *Charles Sumner and the Coming of the Civil War.* New York: Knopf, 1960.

——— (Ed.). *Divided We Fought: A Pictorial History of the Civil War, 1861–1865.* New York: Macmillan, 1959.

Golden Book of the Civil War. New York: Golden Press, 1961.

NEVINS, ALLAN. *Ordeal of the Union.* 2 vols. New York: Scribner's, 1947.

SOBOL, DONALD J. (Ed.). *A Civil War Sampler.* New York: Watts, 1961

STRONG, GEORGE TEMPLETON. *Diary of the Civil War.* Ed. by Allan Nevins. New York: Macmillan, 1962.

Fiction

BENÉT, STEPHEN VINCENT. *John Brown's Body.* New York: Rinehart.

CRANE, STEPHEN. *The Red Badge of Courage.* New York: Macmillan.

KANTOR, MacKINLAY. *Andersonville.* New York: World, 1955.

MITCHELL, MARGARET. *Gone with the Wind.* New York: Macmillan.

INDEX

Anderson, Major Robert, U.S.A., 11

Army of the Potomac, composition of, 18; in Washington, 16. *See also* Union Army

Beauregard, General Pierre G. T., C.S.A., awaits attack at Manassas Junction, 14, 18, 19, 21, 30; and Fort Sumter, 8, 11; at Henry House Hill, 70; and Johnston, 43, 84; refuses to attack Washington, 84; shifts troops, 53, 57; and strategy at Bull Run, 43–44, 50, 51; tries to stem rout, 66

Bee, General Barnard E., C.S.A., 39; at Henry House Hill, 57, 58, 60, 61, 62, 63, 65, 66; killed at Bull Run, 67; troops flee, 83; troops rally, 68, 69

Blackburn's Ford, 38–39, 52, 56

Blenker, Colonel Louis, U.S.A., 85

Bull Run, casualty lists at, 86; Federals open fire at, 35; Johnston moves on, 33, 34, 42; lessons of, 60–71; opening phases of, 50–60; planning for, 18–21; Rebels break at, 64–66; Rebels open fire at, 38–39; retreat, rout, and panic of Union Army at, 68–71, 78–83; South's reaction to, 91–92; spectators at, 47; terrain of, 18; Union Army moves toward, 22–30

Centerville, Va., 54; Colonel Miles at, 81; Federals flee toward, 80; McDowell retreats to, 78; main units of Union Army at, 38

Chinn House and Road, 69, 71

Cooper, General Joseph, C.S.A., 33

Davis, Jefferson, at Bull Run, 84; inaugurated, 10; to Manassas, 47

Early, Colonel Jubal, C.S.A., 42, 54, 69, 78, 84

Ewell, General Richard S., C.S.A., 39, 54

Fairfax Court House, Va., 18, 54; spectators at, 47; Union Army at, 30

Favill, Lieutenant Josiah, U.S.A., describes rout of Federals at Bull Run, 78–79; report of, 90

4th Alabama, 68–69

Grant, General Ulysses S., U.S.A., 93

Greeley, Horace, 16, 50

Heintzelman, General Samuel Peter, U.S.A., 45

Henry, Judith, death of, 60, 87

Henry House Hill, fighting at, 51, 57–60, 61–62, 66–71, 79, 87, 89

Highlanders, 89

Jackson, General Thomas J. ("Stonewall"), C.S.A., 66; at Bull Run, 44; earns nickname "Stonewall," 57, 67–68, 71; at Henry House Hill, 57, 60; at staff meeting at Bull Run, 39; urges immediate attack on Washington, 84

Johnston, General Joseph E., C.S.A., 14, 19, 68; and Beauregard, 42, 43, 54, 66, 83–84; at Bull Run, 51; moves to Manassas Junction, 33–34, 42; shifts men, 57; and strategy at Bull Run, 43–44

Jones, General David R., C.S.A., at Bull Run, 54

Keyes, General Erasmus, U.S.A., 28, 45

Kirby-Smith, General Edmund, C.S.A., 42, 54, 69, 78, 84

Lee, General Robert E., C.S.A., 93

Lincoln, Abraham, attempts to